Letts
Christopher Martin

English

11–14

CONTENTS

FICTION

1. Prose fiction: general
2. Young fiction: post-1914
3. Prose fiction: short stories
4. Prose fiction pre-1914: *Little Women*
5. Prose fiction pre-1914: the Brontës
6. Prose fiction pre-1914: Dickens
7. Prose fiction pre-1914: Sherlock Holmes
8. Prose fiction pre-1914: *The Withered Arm*
9. Prose fiction post-1914: Tolkien
10. Prose fiction post-1914: *Animal Farm*
11. Myth/legend: *Beowulf*
12. Folklore and myth: multicultural

POETRY

13. Poetry: techniques
14. Poetry: narrative
15. Poetry: sonnets
16. Poetry: haiku
17. Poetry: lyric
18. Poetry pre-1914: Blake
19. Poetry pre-1914: Coleridge
20. Poetry pre-1914: Wordsworth
21. Poetry post-1914: Sassoon
22. Poetry post-1914: Owen
23. Poetry post-1914: Auden
24. Poetry post-1914: Heaney

DRAMA

25. Drama: history
26. Drama: history
27. Theatre: history
28. Drama: activities
29. Drama: activities

30 Drama: games
31 Drama: activities
32 Drama: activities
33 Drama post-1914: Priestley
34 Drama: plays

SHAKESPEARE

35 Shakespeare: life and times
36 Shakespeare: the Globe
37 Shakespeare: plays
38 Shakespeare: sonnets
39 Shakespeare: SATs
40 Shakespeare: SATs
41 Shakespeare: SATs

NON-FICTION

42 Non-fiction pre-1914: reportage
43 Non-fiction post-1914: reportage
44 Non-fiction pre-1914: diary
45 Non-fiction post-1914: diary
46 Non-fiction: autobiography
47 Non-fiction: biography
48 Non-fiction: letters
49 Non-fiction: journalism

MEDIA

50 Film: history
51 Film: genre
52 Film: study
53 Comics
54 Magazines
55 Newspapers: history
56 Newspapers
57 Television: history

CONTENTS

58 Television: soap operas
59 Television: news
60 Radio: history
61 Radio
62 Propaganda
63 Advertising

LANGUAGE

64 History of English
65 English: history/variants
66 Spelling
67 Spelling
68 Punctuation
69 Punctuation
70 Grammar: parts of speech
71 Sentences
72 Grammar: general

REFERENCE

73 Dictionary
74 Dictionary of literature
75 Thesaurus
76 Encyclopedia
77 Great writers

SATS REVISION

78 SATs: reading
79 SATs: writing
80 SATs: general

WORD LEVEL

81 Vocabulary
82 Vocabulary: skills
83 Word origins

SENTENCE LEVEL

- **84** Sentence construction
- **85** Paragraphs
- **86** Style
- **87** Standard English

TEXT LEVEL: READING

- **88** Reading for research
- **89** Reading for meaning
- **90** Writer's craft
- **91** Studying texts

TEXT LEVEL: WRITING

- **92** Writing: planning/drafting
- **93** Writing to imagine
- **94** Writing to inform
- **95** Writing to persuade
- **96** Writing to review

SPEAKING AND LISTENING

- **97** Speaking and listening
- **98** Great speeches
- **99** Discussion

GENERAL

- **100** English: general
- **101** Reference

Thanks to Pat and Andy Martin for their advice.

PREFACE

A famous poet once described exploring knowledge as being like walking into a range of mountains. You climb a peak and think that you have reached the top, but then another peak looms in front. When you climb that, there's another ahead ... The computer has given us another comparison: knowledge is like a spider's web. You follow a thread to a junction, then other threads lead away. It's a good metaphor for that huge invisible body of knowledge that we can now bring to our computer screens with the click of a mouse.

Everyone who explores the web knows how uneven it is in quality. There are wonderful sites – rich, up-to-date and full of stunning pictures. Just look at the sites listed here for Shakespeare's sonnets, *Titanic* newspapers, Wilfred Owen or film history. Then there are the useful sites, not much to look at but solid and practical. Finally, there is the sea of advertising and junk sites in which you can so easily be lost!

This book tries to sort out 101 sites that will help Key Stage Three students with their English work. There's some good background here for fiction and non-fiction poems, plays and Shakespeare. There's lots about the media, and there are plenty of sites to help you with those unappealing aspects of English: spelling, punctuation, grammar and SATs!

Bring the amazing treasures of the web into your home and classroom. You love 'surfing' anyway, so why not surf with a purpose? These sites are useful and fun – and they'll help you improve all your English skills.

INTRODUCTION

Introducing Red Hot English Websites

The internet is a fantastic resource for you as a Key Stage 3 English student. Your teacher knows this – which is why you have a copy of this book.

Red Hot English Websites contains directions to the best sites to help you with your English lessons. Your teacher will let you know which sites to visit and when to visit them.

How to use this book

The websites listed in this book have been divided into English sections and topics. These match the topics you will be covering in school. Look at the contents list on pages ii to v for a quick overview of what these topic areas are.

You will see these icons on the pages:

This tells you how to get from the main index of each site to the page you really need. It tells you what to click.

Why should you go there? This section explains what's useful about the site.

Look at this section to discover our top tips and how to apply this website in your school work.

Here you will find details of any additional sites which deal with the same topic.

Don't take our word for it! This section lets you know what other Key Stage 3 students really thought of the site.

Get involved

If you want to give us your feedback on these sites, visit our website: www.letts-education.com/englishwebsites
Your comments will be updated each term so you can keep track of the best internet resources for you and your English lessons.

Safety Notice!

Whilst Letts has made all reasonable enquiries to ensure all the third party websites listed in this publication and accessible via hyperlinks (or otherwise) are suitable for KS3 students, Letts Educational does not endorse or approve the content of any such third party websites nor does it accept any responsibility or liability for their content. Further, Letts makes no warranty or representation about anything contained in any such third party websites referred to herein or that can be accessed by hyperlink (or otherwise) nor that their URLs will continue to be maintained, available and accessible and accepts no liability in connection with any suggestion or claim that any such third party website breaches any law or regulation or in any other way infringes any of your rights. Also, you acknowledge that internet sites can change very quickly and Letts Educational accepts no responsibility or liability for any subsequent changes to the contents of any such third party websites, their URLs and/or any other online material.

Letts Educational strongly advises teachers, parents, and/or guardians to access, review and monitor all such third party websites before directing students to them and also generally for schools actively to encourage parental supervision of students who are accessing the internet at home.

Prose fiction: general

www.novelguide.com

 Choose from the list of books, then select an approach under **Choose to Continue**.

 Useful summaries, character studies and valuable brief biographies of authors. Have a look at the **Top Ten Quotes**. You may not agree with the **Theme Analysis** or **Metaphor Analysis** sections but they will start you thinking about the deeper meanings of the novels.

 This site will give you ideas and a good structure for a general wide reading book report. But don't forget that you will need to add your personal responses and opinions too.

 www.bibliomania.com

 The Top Ten Quotes saved me from looking through the whole book.

Young fiction: post-1914

YEAR 7/8

 How to use it
 Look out for
 Hints
 Other links
 Student comments

www.achuka.co.uk

 Choose from the colourful menu on top of the home page. **Teen/YA, Fic** (Fiction), **Profiles** and especially **Interviews** are the most use.

 The latest news about books for young readers. The list of awards and shortlists will help you discover new authors and titles. The profiles, interviews, and photographs bring you closer to the writers and their books.

 Try the interviews with Bernard Ashley: *Johnnie's Blitz*; Philip Pullman: *The Subtle Knife*; Kevin Crossley Holland: *King Arthur* or Michael Morpurgo: *Stories from Hereabouts Hill*. They will whet your appetite for reading!

 www.lib.lsu.edu/hum/authors.html

 It looks smart, up-to-date and colourful. It makes you want to read.

 How to use it
 Look out for
 Hints
 Other links
 Student comments

YEAR 8/9

Prose fiction: short stories

cityofshadows.stegenga.net

 The homepage offers you a creepy Gothic Tour of Victorian London. Then choose **A Dark Night's Work** to find the ghost stories.

 With its dark headings and sinister old photos, this site looks delightfully chilling! The stories are mostly written in fairly complicated 19th-century English but be patient and read on. Try Elizabeth Braddon, Charles Dickens, M.R. James or W.W. Jacobs for really spine-tingling moments. In **The Haunted** section, you will find details of Borley Rectory, supposedly the most haunted house in England.

 A reading project on pre- and post-1914 ghost stories would be exciting. Look at the author biographies under **Through a Glass Darkly**.

 atoledo.freeyellow.com/stories.html
Horror stories
www.channel4.com/learning/main/secondary
Click on **English** and scroll down to **Hooked on Horror**.

YEAR 7/8

Prose fiction pre-1914: *Little Women*

How to use it | Look out for | Hints | Other links | Student comments

www.alcottweb.com

 This is all about Louisa May Alcott, author of *Little Women*. Read the lively home page then click on **Writing** for texts and discussions of her work, and on **Picture Gallery** for images of the author, her family and her home.

 You won't need the whole text of *Little Women* (available to read here) but some of the other writing will be useful. *Little Women* is set in Orchard House, which you can see in the Picture Gallery.

 Go to **LMA Today**. Scroll down to find a review called Little Women: the Movie. This review of the 1994 film is a good model for your own writing. You could compare the film and the novel in a reading project on Louisa May Alcott.

 www.empirezine.com/spotlight/alcott/alcott.htm

 I liked seeing the old American house where *Little Women* is set.

How to use it | Look out for | Hints | Other links | Student comments

www.bronte.info

This is the official Brontë Society site, so it's expert and informative. Go to **The Brontës**, then to **Who Were the Brontës?**, **Family Tree** and **The Novels**.

There are some fine illustrations here, often done by the amazing Brontë sisters themselves. The family history is fascinating and the novel outlines are good for pre-reading. The **Museum** gives you a tour of the Parsonage, the home that meant so much to the sisters. There is the dining table that they walked round as they invented their novels – and there are their tiny personal writing desks.

Use in a study project of the Brontës and their work, or to prepare for a visit to the Parsonage Museum in Haworth.

www.lang.nagoya-u.ac.jp/~matsuoka/Bronte.html

YEAR 8/9

Prose fiction pre-1914: Dickens

www.fidnet.com/~dap1955/dickens

 This is a fine survey of Dickens, his world and his writing. Go to **The Novels** and then click on the book you want from the shelf. Also look at **Dickens' London**.

 This site really makes you want to read Dickens by cleverly choosing passages to show you the writer's 'unbounded imagination'. The novel guide gives you lively mini-outlines, and notes on Dickens' amazing characters. The interactive map of 1859 London allows you to explore streets and alleys in the city of contrasting wealth and 'untold squalor and filth' that Dickens described so well.

 A project on Dickens and his 19th-century world would be a good preparation for reading a complete novel or some of the short stories. If you are reading *A Christmas Carol*, then find out about **Dickens & Christmas** from this site.

 www.dickensmuseum.com
The Dickens House Museum in London.

 The old map was nice to play around with.

YEAR 7/8

Prose fiction pre-1914: Sherlock Holmes

www.sherlockian.net

 This is a good general site about Sherlock Holmes and Sir Arthur Conan Doyle. The most useful pages are **The Original Sherlock Holmes Stories**, **The World of Holmes and Watson** and **Sherlockian Resources on the Web**.

 You can find lots of background to the famous detective stories here, or you can read them online. There is also a plan of 221b Baker Street; details of Moriarty, Holmes' arch enemy; information about *Strand* magazine, where the stories first appeared and there is plenty about Doyle himself – even about the Cottingley Fairy hoax that tricked him.

 If you're going to read the stories or *The Hound of the Baskervilles*, then prepare a background project first.

 www.sherlock-holmes.co.uk
The Sherlock Holmes Museum.
www.online-literature.com/doyle

 The links section is very good, taking you deeper and deeper.

How to use it — Look out for — Hints — Other links — Student comments

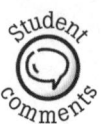

www.learn.co.uk

Go to **Key Stage 4** **English Literature – Prose**. Some of this material is also suitable for KS3. Then go to **The Withered Arm and Other Wessex Tales**.

First you'll need to read Thomas Hardy's story, with its strange little chapters. Then study **Background to the Tales** with its map of 'the ancient kingdom of Wessex' and its description of the old country way of life. The notes remind you of useful literary terms, such as 'narrator', 'setting' and 'context'. The discussion is wide-ranging but strongest on characterisation.

You can learn a lot about short story technique from this clear guide. It helps you to pick evidence from the text so that you can support your points effectively. It will also help you to write your own short story.

www.channel4.com/learning/main/secondary
Click on **English** and scroll down to **Classic Short Prose**.

www.tolkiensociety.org/tolkien/index.html

 Go to **A Biography of J.R.R. Tolkien**, **Books by Tolkien** or **Tolkien as a Writer for Young Adults**.

 As *The Lord of the Rings* was voted 'Book of the 20th century', there are many weird and wonderful sites on Tolkien but this is the official site. The biography reminds us of how Tolkien began writing his Elvish languages in the Somme trenches of 1916. Tolkien as a Writer for Young Adults explains the writing of the book, and how its paperback edition created a huge young readership for the novel.

 You may have seen the film of *The Lord of the Rings* but now it's time to read the book – it's long but unforgettable. This site will guide you. Start with *The Hobbit*, of course.

 www.csclub.uwaterloo.ca/u/relipper/tolkien/rootpage.html

 I hoped there'd be more pictures but the life story was interesting.

 How to use it
 Look out for
 Hints
 Other links
 Student comments

www.novelguide.com/animalfarm

This is a guide to George Orwell's *Animal Farm*, one of the best-selling books of the 20th century. Use the menu on the home page for **Novel Summary**, **Character Profiles**, **Theme Analysis** and **Metaphor Analysis**. Start with the **Biography** of Orwell.

Orwell called this a 'fairy tale' but it is actually a dark protest against some of the worst tendencies of the 20th century. It's a book that needs a lot of background explanation and this site gives you plenty. The theme and metaphor discussions are particularly well-handled.

The exploration of the double meanings in this apparently simple story will give you a wonderful insight into the power of literature.

www.spartacus.schoolnet.co.uk/Jorwell.htm

This helped a lot with history and reading.

 How to use it
 Look out for
 Hints
 Other links
 Student comments

YEAR 7

Myth/legend: *Beowulf*

www.lone-star.net/literature/beowulf/index.html

The home page gives useful background to *Beowulf* with a picture of the only (slightly burned) manuscript. Go to **The Adventure Begins Here!**

The 1000-year-old *Beowulf* is the oldest classic narrative poem in English literature. You study it here in a modern translation. On this site, the best parts of the story are put into lively, easily-read English – the original is written in Anglo-Saxon! The pictures are good, inspired by Anglo-Saxon relics dug up at Sutton Hoo in Suffolk.

Do your own description of Grendel. You'll need to add a picture. If you can, compare this translation with others, such as *Dragonslayer* (Sutclif) or *Beowulf* (Heaney).

www.thecomic.com/beowulf.html
Exciting samples from a graphic novel version of the story!

Where can I get the comic? It's great!

Folklore and myth: multicultural

teacher.scholastic.com/writewit/mff/myths_home.htm

 Under the heading **Activities** go to **Myths from Around the World**.

 This is a very thorough survey of story-telling in myth and folklore from many parts of the world. Explore some of the stories. Some, such as those of Greece or Rome, you probably know. Try somewhere new: Australia, Celtic lands, or North America. You get a sample story and some explanation, and the pictures are very striking.

 Go back to **Activities** on the original page and try **Myth Writing with Jane Yolen**. She'll tell you how to write your own myth. The warm-up is good for your general writing skills.

 www.darsie.net/talesofwonder

 The workshop was fun. I'd like to try writing a myth now.

YEAR 8/9

Poetry: techniques

> www.learn.co.uk

 Go to **Key Stage 3** **English Literature – Poetry** and then to **Introduction to Poetry**.

 This clear site explains the technical features of poetry that you should know about. Look at **Activity 1** and **Activity 2** which remind you of key words about poetic forms. Then go back to the previous page to read over **Language in Poetry**, which revises figures of speech, rhyme etc. Difficult concepts such as metaphor are particularly well-explained.

 The site is interactive so try to answer some questions to check that you understand the ideas. There are good reference and revision points here but you'll need to bring them alive by looking closely at actual poems.

 www.geocities.com/~spanoudi/poems
Provides a useful index to poems and poets.

 Helps you to understand the technical terms.

13

Poetry: narrative

YEAR 7/8

www.learn.co.uk

Go to **Key Stage 3** **English Literature – Poetry** then choose **Narrative Poetry**.

Narrative poems are stories in verse so it's hard squeezing them into the small space available on a webite. Even so, the extracts – from *How they Brought the Good News from Ghent to Aix* (Browning) and *The Listeners* (De la Mare) – are gripping. Best is the excellent analysis of the complete *Out, Out* (Frost). The colour highlights on technical points are useful.

The comprehension questions on the poems are stretching, though the suggestion to 'write your own narrative poem' is unrealistic. Writing an opening or a part of such a poem would be more suitable.

etext.lib.virginia.edu/stc/Coleridge/poems/Rime_Ancient_Mariner.html
The full text of a great narrative poem, with notes.

Poetry: sonnets

YEAR 8/9

www.learn.co.uk

Go to **Key Stage 3** **English Literature – Poetry** then select **Sonnets**.

Sonnets are good to study because they are so compact and have been written in so many eras of English poetry. This site reminds you about sonnet forms. The examples: *Sonnet 130* (Shakespeare), *O Earth, lie heavily* (Rossetti), *Batter my heart* (Donne), and *The Fly* (Reid), are discussed thoughtfully.

The final activity is to write your own sonnet. The instruction is vague and the writing difficult, but it can be done! If it seems too hard, just write your own ideas about one or two of the sonnets instead.

www.sonnets.org
Try **The Sonnet in Great Britain** – a wonderful collection.

Poetry: haiku

YEAR 7

How to use it · Look out for · Hints · Other links · Student comments

www.learn.co.uk

Go to **Key Stage 3** **English Literature – Poetry** then select **The Haiku**, **Clerihew**, **Limerick** and **Shape**.

This is a lively, colourful site which helps you to write short poems. The haiku is clearly explained (with some lovely Japanese paintings). The examples are fresh and the questions make you think hard about the forms. The clerihew, limericks and shapes are fun, too.

The shape poems are interesting to try. If you've done haikus before, why not try a haiku sequence? You could do one for each season, or for each month of the year, for example.

www.toyomasu.com/haiku
Lots more haikus. Look closely at Basho's – he's the master!

I liked all the colours and the ideas for writing.

How to use it | Look out for | Hints | Other links | Student comments

YEAR 8/9

Poetry: lyric

www.learn.co.uk

Go to **Key Stage 3** **English Literature – Poetry** then choose **The Lyric**.

'Lyric' is an off-putting word but there's a good explanation here (with a picture of a lyre!). Heaney's *A Drink of Water* is discussed well, with colour-coded notes, exploring the points you revised earlier (page 13). Then you can study an interesting selection: *The Lesson* (Lucie-Smith), *Daffodils* (Wordsworth), and *The Windhover* (Hopkins).

The activities make you reflect and work. You could certainly try to write your own lyric as is suggested here. Why not do 'A remembered experience' like the Wordsworth poem?

www.shunsley.eril.net/armoore/contents.htm
More useful guides to poetry under
English Language/Literature KS2/3.

17

Poetry pre-1914: Blake

YEAR 8/9

www.shunsley.eril.net/armoore/poetry/blake.htm

 Read the good **Introduction**, then use the menu at the top of the page to select individual poems.

 Blake is a brilliant poet, whose work looks easy but is difficult to understand fully. Famous and mysterious poems like *The Tyger*, *A Poison Tree* and *London* are effectively discussed here. The questioning forces you to puzzle ideas out for yourself. Key words and images are a special part of Blake and here the notes are very useful.

 Take a pair of poems to compare and contrast: *The Tyger* and *The Lamb* are extraordinary opposites. Do your own Blake-style illuminated copies of the poems before you start.

 www.tate.org.uk/britain/exhibitions/blakeinteractive
This shows you some of Blake's beautiful illuminated pages.

YEAR 8/9

Poetry pre-1914: Coleridge

www.shunsley.eril.net/armoore/poetry/mariner.htm

Start with the **Introduction** and follow through or choose from headings at the top of the page.

Coleridge's *The Rime of the Ancient Mariner* is magical but can be off-putting because it's so long. This study guide takes you through the poem thoughtfully, with useful background and stimulating activities. The more advanced **Examining the Text** section helps pupils to compare the 1798 and 1817 versions of the poem. Themes and imagery are dealt with quite fully.

The Ship's Log and **Map-making** look like really exciting activities. **Performing the Poem** is also a great idea!

For full text go to **Click Here** at the beginning of the Introduction or try
etext.lib.virginia.edu/stc/Coleridge/poems/Rime_Ancient_Mariner.html

19

YEAR 8/9

Poetry pre-1914: Wordsworth

 How to use it
 Look out for
 Hints
 Other links
 Student comments

www.wordsworth.org.uk/dovecottage

Try `Guided Tour`, `Children's Guide` or `Dorothy's Grasmere Journal`.

Dove Cottage is the home of the Wordsworth Museum. The poet lived and worked here with his sister, Dorothy. He wrote poems while she recorded their daily life in her journals. Take the tour of the house and garden. See the rooms where they were so happy and creative. Notice the 'Children's room' that Dorothy papered with newspaper!

Read the excellent `Story of Dove Cottage`, in the children's guide. You could then do a short project on Dove Cottage as an introduction to reading the poems.

www.shunsley.eril.net/armoore/contents.htm
Go to the tutorial on Wordsworth's *And in the frosty season* under `English Language/Literature KS2/3`.

 How to use it
 Look out for
 Hints
 Other links
 Student comments

YEAR 9

Poetry post-1914: Sassoon

www.geocities.com/CapitolHill/8103/index.html

 Read the biography of Siegfried Sassoon. Then go to **Poetry of War as a Noble Enterprise** and **War as a Pointless and Wasteful Endeavour** for the poems. On this second page also click on **A Soldier's Declaration**, Sassoon's open letter of protest against the Great War.

 Sassoon's fierce, deadly satires on battle and war hit you hard. There is a good selection of his angry poems here such as *The Rear-Guard* and *Does it Matter?* Dazzling war paintings are presented beside the poems.

 Use this site in a study of Sassoon himself, or in a general war poetry project. You might try linking the poetry and the paintings of the Western Front.

 www.art-ww1.com/gb/peintre.html
A hundred brilliant paintings and drawings from the First World War.

 It really helps to look at the poems and pictures together.

Poetry post-1914: Owen

www.wilfred.owen.association.mcmail.com

Try the **Virtual Tour** to see places that were important in Owen's life. Then use the **His Poetry** link for lots of information on all his famous poems. Select the poem you want to study and after reading the commentary click on **Poem Text**.

When you have read the poem text, click on **Manuscript Sources**. Look, for example, at the manuscript versions of *Dulce Et Decorum Est* and *Futility*. This allows you to follow the changes made by Owen, giving you a wonderful sense of how the poems were formed.

This information would be useful in a short study of Owen, or in a general project on Great War poets. The site links to useful material on Siegfried Sassoon, Rupert Brooke, Edmund Blunden, Edward Thomas and Ivor Gurney.

www.bbc.co.uk/history/war/wwone/index.shtml
This site gives valuable background on the First World War.

Really cool to see the poems in Owen's handwriting with crossings out and changes.

How to use it

Look out for

Hints

Other links

Student comments

YEAR **7/8**

Poetry post-1914: Auden

www.shunsley.eril.net/armoore/poetry/classics.htm#5

Read the background notes, then **How is it Written?** and move on to **Other Responses**.

Auden's poem about the night mail train to Scotland is justly famous for its amazing rhythm effects. You'll need a copy of the poem to explore this site. See the film, as well, with its music by Benjamin Britten. The analysis is useful, but try to think carefully yourself about the train rhythms built into the language.

Performing the Poem makes some good suggestions. You could break the poem down to read round the class. Writing about a journey could be interesting, too.

www.editor.net/griersontrust/nightmail/nightmail.htm
This has pictures, words and music from the film.

Poetry post-1914: Heaney

YEAR 9

www.shunsley.eril.net/armoore/poetry/heaney.htm

 Choose individual poems for study from the list at the top of the page.

 Seamus Heaney is a Nobel Prize winner and is considered by many to be the greatest living poet writing in English. You should certainly read some of his poems. This is a short but close study of six well-known poems, including *Follower*, *Digging* and *Mid-Term Break*, for which you will need texts. The discussion is strong on metaphors and language effects.

 Try some of the suggested comparisons of paired poems that share a theme.

 www.ibiblio.org/ipa/heaney
Listen to Heaney reading some of his poems!

 This helped quite a lot with the ideas of the poems.

Drama: history

www.ebicom.net/~tct/history.htm

This deals with drama from ancient times to the 20th century. Click on **Ancient**, **Shakespeare** and **Since Will**.

This is an informative and expert site on all aspects of drama history. It gives you the essential points about theatre design, playwrights and plays for each era. The pictures are valuable.

You might need this site for drama studies if you are doing a research project on some aspects of theatrical history – it's a useful starting place.

www.emory.edu/ENGLISH/DRAMA/Hist Drama1.html
Unfinished but exciting: nice drama film clips to look at.

I thought the Greek theatre looked interesting.

Drama: history

YEAR 7/8

 How to use it
 Look out for
 Hints
 Other links
 Student comments

didaskalia.berkeley.edu/Didintro.html

 Make your way through the short chapters, then go to **Introduction to Greek Stagecraft** and **Introduction to Roman Stagecraft**.

 It's a good idea to know how theatre began. This site deals with the beginnings of drama in Greece and Rome. There are lovely pictures and diagrams. It's nice to find out where the words 'thespian', 'orchestra' and 'satire' come from. The sections on **The Players** and **Masks** are particularly good. Look at the interactive mask model, and put its wig on and off! The three-dimensional theatre models are very stimulating.

 Do a study comparing Shakespeare's theatre with that of Ancient Greece.

 www.yorkearlymusic.org/mysteryplays/index.htm
This covers early church drama in England.

 The models and masks are fun to look at.

26

Theatre: history

YEAR 8/9

How to use it · Look out for · Hints · Other links · Student comments

theatremuseum.vam.ac.uk/index.htm

How to use it: Read the introduction, then use the menu on the left-hand side of the screen to move around the site.

Look out for: The National Theatre Museum in London is important for any study you make of theatre history. **Collections and Research** details the vast range of theatrical treasures that may be studied in the museum.

Hints: The video archive, which can only be seen at the museum but is described here, shows scenes from great past productions. You mustn't miss this site in your drama work.

Other links: www.ebicom.net/~tct/sincewill.htm

Student comments: The videos sound interesting.

27

Drama: activities

YEAR 9

How to use it · *Look out for* · *Hints* · *Other links* · *Student comments*

www.geocities.com/Broadway/Alley/3765/lessons.html

How to use it: On main menu, go to `Lesson Plans Sorted by Age Level`. Items for older pupils tend to be later in the list.

Look out for: This is about creative drama and children's theatre. There are drama lesson plans and playlets, created by a playwright and teacher. Start with `Improvs and Warm-ups`. Try `Job Interview`, `Concept Charades`, `Paper Masks`, `The Discovery of Fire` or `Oregon Trail Propaganda`. There are so many good ideas here.

Hints: The Improvs and Warm-ups will get you going and give you confidence.

Other links: www.prism.gatech.edu/~gt4510b/improv/index.html

Student comments: We tried some of the ideas in class. They're fun.

Drama: activities

How to use it · *Look out for* · *Hints* · *Other links* · *Student comments*

YEAR 9

www.hi8us.co.uk

How to use it: Click on **Current Projects**, on the cabinet drawers, then on the files. Choose the file called **Edrama**.

Look out for: This is an exciting, ambitious and still-developing site, packed with good practical ideas. The centrepiece is the Edrama project, where young people will be able to create their own dramas and scripts. Virtual characters will be performed by virtual actors.

Hints: You can plan ideas for plays in a most imaginative way. If you are a little shy but full of lively ideas, this site will suit you well. **Edrama for Careers** is interesting, too.

Other links: www.geocities.com/Broadway/Alley/3765/lessons.html
Lots more activity ideas.

Drama: games

YEAR: All

- How to use it
- Look out for
- Hints
- Other links
- Student comments

> www.bced.gov.bc.ca/irp/drama810/apg.htm

How to use it: This is an appendix to a larger drama site. Scroll down the extensive list of games and read whatever interests you.

Look out for: This is a splendidly imaginative and varied set of games designed to get you moving and talking in drama. Try them – they will give you confidence!

Hints: You'll want to test them in class or with friends. Try `Day in the Life of ...`, `Eye-to-Eye Argument` and `Frozen Pictures`. Enjoy them and develop your skills!

Other links:
expage.com/page/dgone
More good drama games.

Student comments: There's so much here and it's going to work well.

Drama: activities

YEAR: All

- 👁️ How to use it
- 👁️ Look out for
- ❗ Hints
- 🖥️ Other links
- 💬 Student comments

www.geocities.com/Shalyndria13/link.htm

👁️ This site calls itself 'the queen of all theatre link sites' and has an amazing range of useful web addresses for all aspects of theatre study and work. Scan the list for what you want.

👁️ Just try sites that fit your special interests. **The Elizabethan Costuming Page** will be useful for Shakespeare productions with its fine set of contemporary portraits and even patterns for clothes. The **Stage Make Up** is amazing.

❗ Try the **Acting Workshop On-Line**. It tells you how to audition for a part and 'what every actor ought to know'.

🖥️ costume.dm.net
members.aol.com/nebula5/costume.html
Two more costume pages.

💬 I loved the make-up and costume ideas.

Drama: activities

How to use it | **Look out for** | **Hints** | **Other links** | **Student comments**

www.shunsley.eril.net/armoore/drama/drama.htm

How to use it: Go through the general points in `Drama at Key Stage 3` in the first column.

Look out for: This site is really for drama teachers but pupils can learn a lot here, too. Go back to the menu for some interesting activities, such as `Ideas for Improvisation`, `Starters and Fill-ups` and two sections on `Games`. `Planning and Scripting a Play` has some good suggestions for short scripts and don't miss `Drama Techniques A–Z`.

Hints: The mime in `Pandora's Box` is intriguing. Try `Chilling Tales` or `Drama and Media – Advertising Campaign`.

Other links: www.teachit.co.uk

YEAR 9

Drama post-1914: Priestley

How to use it | *Look out for* | *Hints* | *Other links* | *Student comments*

> www.shunsley.eril.net/armoore/drama/inspectorcalls.htm

How to use it: This takes you straight to the tutorial on J.B. Priestley.

Look out for: J.B. Priestley's *An Inspector Calls* is often a GCSE study text but you might do it in Year 9. You need to read the play first, or see the black and white film. The tasks will really help in the study of the play. There's lots of clear, well-ordered and imaginative information including the valuable 'time scheme' of the play.

Hints: The follow-up ideas are exciting. **Eva's Letter**, **The Media Version**, **Who Is To Blame?** and **Responsibility** are all stimulating pieces of work suitable for your coursework folder.

Other links: www.kirjasto.sci.fi/priestle.htm
Useful quotations and very helpful for the author's life and work.

Student comments: We went to see the play in London and this helped us to prepare.

Drama: plays

www.theatrehistory.com

How to use it: Choose which era of theatre you want, then go to the theme or author you need.

Look out for: This site is rather commercial-looking but there is plenty of information here about theatre, plays and playwrights. Try Oscar Wilde, under (Irish Theatre) for example. You get a good biography and a useful outline of *The Importance of Being Earnest*. The (On-line Texts) of complete plays could also be useful.

Hints: The short one-act or ten-minute plays would be just the thing for drama lessons. The set of monologues would help you in auditions.

Other links: www.geocities.com/Shalyndria13/link.htm
Links galore!

Student comments: My friend and I are going to try one of the short plays.

Shakespeare: life and times

www.shakespeare.org.uk

How to use it: Use the general menu on the title page.

Look out for: This is an introduction to Shakespeare's life and work in Stratford and London. This Shakespeare Birthplace Trust site is wonderfully thorough, expert and up-to-date. The key facts and documents are all here with excellent pictures, some of them surprisingly fresh. I liked the reconstructions of the Shakespeare houses. The virtual Tour, showing the new decorations for the Millennium, is very exciting.

Hints: If you're doing a general project on Shakespeare before starting the SATs play, or going to see one of his plays in the theatre, then start with this site.

Other links:
shakespeare.eb.com
Beautifully illustrated. Good on film and music.

Student comments: I liked virtual-touring Shakespeare's house. I must go there!

Shakespeare: the Globe

www.rdg.ac.uk/globe

How to use it: Click on **Shakespeare's Globe**, then on individual items in the **Index for the Original Globe**. The excellent pictures can be enlarged – just click on them.

Look out for: This is an expert survey of Elizabethan theatres and it includes material on the **New Globe** of today. The detail is excellent and the pictures often entirely new. The **Illustrations** showing panoramas of old London are fascinating. You can explore the remains of the real Rose and Globe. Try the useful map on:
London Playhouses in the 16th and 17th Centuries.

Hints: A project on the Globe, both old and new, would be a fine introduction to Shakespeare for the SATs.

Other links:
www.shakespeares-globe.org
The official website of the reconstructed Shakespeare's Globe Theatre.
www.bardweb.net/globe.html
Useful pictures.

Student comments: Everything you need to know about the Globe is here!

Shakespeare: plays

How to use it • **Look out for** • **Hints** • **Other links** • **Student comments**

> **the-tech.mit.edu/Shakespeare**

🖱️ The complete works of Shakespeare online: simply choose a title from the main menu lists under **Comedy**, **History** and **Tragedy**. Then click on the **Act** and **Scene** you want.

👁️ This is very easy to use and the text is extremely clear. It's almost quicker than leafing through a book of the collected plays! This is going to be particularly useful if you've left your book at school or if you have to share a copy.

❗ A very useful stand-by when you are doing essays and projects, and you want to find quotations to support your ideas.

💻 shakespeare.palomar.edu
A full range of Shakespeare sites: brilliant!

💬 The plays are easy to find and easy to read.

Shakespeare: sonnets

www.shakespeares-sonnets.com

How to use it: Read the **Advice on Using this Site**. You will be able to select the sonnet you want if you know the number. Alternatively scroll through them all, or even do a search on the first line or a single phrase.

Look out for: This is one of the finest literature sites online. All the sonnets are here, with others by Shakespeare's contemporaries. There are also splendid 16th and 17th century illustrations. The facsimiles of some poems let you see the sonnets as they were first printed in the pirated edition of 1609 (with all its puzzles about Mr W.H.!).

Hints: If you choose a sonnet for close study, then use the excellent commentary (click on the number above the sonnet).

Other links:
www.Iloveshakespeare.com
More about the Dark Lady mystery.

Student comments: The pictures make this site really exciting.

Shakespeare: SATs

How to use it | **Look out for** | **Hints** | **Other links** | **Student comments**

YEAR 9

www.learn.co.uk

Go to **Key Stage 3** **English Literature – Drama**. Then click on your set play.

These clear notes are really going to help you do well in your Shakespeare SATs paper. Each play has a background, brief notes on character and a story outline. The Acts and Scenes have excellent commentaries, both in outline and in detail. The tests are fun and make you concentrate, and the exam tips are valuable.

These notes are going to help you when you start your set play and when you're doing last-minute revision. They're not going to replace your own close study in class but they will definitely support your work and help you get a good grade.

www.teachit.co.uk

Very, very helpful.

Shakespeare: SATs

YEAR 9

- How to use it
- Look out for
- Hints
- Other links
- Student comments

www.bbc.co.uk/education/ks3bitesize

How to use it: Go to **Choose a Subject** and, under **English**, select **Shakespeare Character**, **Shakespeare Dramatic Effect** or **Shakespeare Summaries**. Then click **Go**.

Look out for: This site is not as detailed as some but it does support the BBC TV lessons. There are brief summaries of the plays but this site concentrates on the set scenes, which are discussed thoroughly.

Hints: The tests are stimulating. If you do well on these, you will be prepared for the SATs paper. The best way to use this site is in quick revision – it will help you feel confident about the exam.

Other links: www.teachit.co.uk/teachit/sats.htm
More revision.

Student comments: This site is good for working on your own to go over the scenes.

Shakespeare: SATs

YEAR 9

- How to use it
- Look out for
- Hints
- Other links
- Student comments

www.teachit.co.uk

How to use it: Go to **Key Stage 3**, then to **Drama**. Pick your set play.

Look out for: This is a large site based on teachers' worksheets – plenty to do on *Twelfth Night*, *Henry V* and *Macbeth*. There are close-focus studies, comprehension passages, notes on direction, puzzles and lots more. You won't use them all but these are useful ideas that will certainly help with the SATs paper.

Hints: The work ideas are full and flexible. Try the sample SATs questions. Explore this large site. There are so many practical ideas here on all sorts of topics.

Student comments: I found some things here helpful for revision.

YEAR 7/8

Non-fiction pre-1914: reportage

How to use it · *Look out for* · *Hints* · *Other links* · *Student comments*

etext.lib.virginia.edu/toc/modeng/public/MayLond.html

- Scroll down the list through the chapters, clicking on items that interest you. Look out for **Two Orphan Flower Girls** in Chapter 7 and the **Watercress Girl** in Chapter 8.

- Henry Mayhew interviewed hundreds of poor people living or working in the London streets of the 1850s. Dickensian London comes alive through these amazing sketches, which reveal the life-stories of obscure people. The plight of poor children is particularly moving.

- Use as a background to a study of Dickens, or for language history. You could take a title or two from the list and write your own interviews with the characters.

- Look up other studies of London's poor (like those of George Sims or Jack London, for example) on the same site.

- It's weird – all these people talking from the past!

How to use it · **Look out for** · **Hints** · **Other links** · **Student comments**

YEAR 9

Non-fiction post-1914: reportage

www.education.bl.uk/projects/index.html

(How to use it) This is a powerful British Library site, excellent for Holocaust studies. Scroll down to **Voices of the Holocaust** and click – **Testimony Library** is the best section.

(Look out for) You can read and listen to the testimony of survivors of concentration camps (use the **play buttons**). **Topic 3: The Camps** is truly terrible but is the more vivid for being expressed as spoken language. The pictures and biographies also help us to respond to these real people.

(Hints) Use with your Holocaust project, or to help with poems on this subject. Try the **Student Worksheets** from **Teachers' Information**.

(Other links) www.iwm.org.uk/lambeth/holo-wit.htm
The Imperial War Museum's Holocaust exhibition.

(Student comments) This really brought home to me what happened to Jews in Hitler's Europe.

43

Non-fiction pre-1914: diary

YEAR 8/9

How to use it · **Look out for** · **Hints** · **Other links** · **Student comments**

> spider.georgetowncollege.edu/
> english/allen/pepys.htm

How to use it: Read Pepys' biographical **Time Line** on this page, then click on **Go to the Diary**. Scroll down to 3 August–7 September 1665 for his entries about the Great Plague. Then scroll further down to 2–7 September 1666 for descriptions, and a painting, of the Great Fire of London.

Look out for: The whole diary is massive but here are some famous passages about the Restoration of Charles II (1660), the Great Plague and the Great Fire of London. Read these and you will understand why Pepys' reportage is so admired.

Hints: Study the passages closely and make notes on Pepys' choice of detail and his sharp observation of events. Compare with John Evelyn's diary description of the Fire.

Other links: www.blackmask.com/books24c/pepysdex.htm
More about the diary.

How to use it | Look out for | Hints | Other links | Student comments

www.annefrank.nl

How to use it: Click on **English** to translate the notes. Then choose **Anne Frank House**, **Anne Frank** and **Diary**.

Look out for: This is the official site of the Anne Frank House Museum in Amsterdam. Anne's brilliant diary has become one of the most widely read books in the world. Follow her brief life, illustrated with impressive photos, some in colour. Tour the rooms of the claustrophobic secret annexe, where the Franks hid from the Nazis for two years. You can see hand-written facsimiles of the Diary and, best of all, you can read quotations from this wonderful writer.

Hints: Use in a study of Holocaust literature, or of Anne Frank herself. The Anne Frank House Museum offers lots of other resources too.

Other links: www.education.bl.uk/projects/index.html
Another fine Holocaust site.

Student comments: This helps you to see the places that you read about in the Diary.

Non-fiction: autobiography

www.ku.edu/~kansite/ww_one/bio/b/brittain.html

How to use it
This is a straightforward summary of Vera Brittain's Great War autobiography, *Testament of Youth*. Simply read through.

Look out for
The site outlines Vera Brittain's comfortable pre-1914 background and describes her trials as a nurse in war-torn France. There is a full description of *Testament of Youth*, with its poignant record of the deaths of young men, including her fiancé, Roland Leighton, and her post-traumatic stress when she returned to university.

Hints
Use this site, Brittain's poetry and the moving *Letters from a Lost Generation*, written by Vera and her friends, in a study of women's experience of the Great War.

Other links
www.wise.virginia.edu/history/wciv2/vera.html
Good extracts from *Testament of Youth*.

Student comments
I already knew a bit about the war poets but not about women in the 1914–18 war.

YEAR 7/8

Non-fiction: biography

- How to use it
- Look out for
- Hints
- Other links
- Student comments

> www.bham.wednet.edu/bio/biomak2.htm

Click on the different sections under **Follow These Steps**.

It is interesting to read about famous people, but a good way to investigate biography is to try writing one yourself. This site will give you a structure for your work. The stages – **Questioning**, **Learning**, **Synthesis** and **Story-telling** – are very practical. You will also need to do some substantial reading research about great lives.

Use the two rich sites below for the following project: 'Produce a short illustrated biography of Jane Austen or William Shakespeare'.

www.pemberley.com/janeinfo/janelife.html
www.shakespeare-online.com/biography

Non-fiction: letters

YEAR 9

- How to use it
- Look out for
- Hints
- Other links
- Student comments

www.bbc.co.uk/history/war/wwone/index.shtml

How to use it: Go to **The Human Face of War**. Then click on individuals such as **The Private** and **The Captain**.

Look out for: Personal letters from the trenches and the Home Front give you a strong sense of the human tragedy of the First World War. The writers are articulate and brave. The letters from the captain, the army chaplain and the mother are the most moving. Listen also to the audio memories of soldiers, which include some letters.

Hints: Use the detail from this fine site to write your own letter from a soldier in the Western Front trenches in 1916.

Other links: info.ox.ac.uk/jtap/tutorials/intro/owen/letters.html
Some famous war letters written by Wilfred Owen.

Student comments: The trench letters give you the reality behind the poetry.

How to use it

www.lva.lib.va.us/whoweare/exhibits/titanic/index.htm

Read the excellent introduction. Then click on **Titanic Exhibit** at the top of the page. Here you can read a review of the newspaper coverage of the disaster. Click on **Passenger List**, **Survivors** and **Headline Coverage** for more detail and photographs.

Look out for

This is a rich and varied archive of 1912 newspaper reports of the sinking of the *Titanic*. It is a treasure trove of journalistic writing about a great event. There are headlines, articles, poems and cartoons. Editors reflect on the mania for speed and luxury, the guilt of the White Star line, and the inadequate lifeboats.

Hints

Do a newspaper front page of your own, describing the disaster, or try a short non-fiction project on the *Titanic*, using some of the evidence here.

Other links

www.irelandseye.com/titanic/disaster.htm
Go to **The Disaster Reported** – click on the newspaper fragments.

Student comments

The film got me interested and this site takes you a lot further into the story.

Film: history

www.filmsite.org

How to use it: Click on **Film History** under **For reference** on the left-hand side of the screen. Go to **History by Decade**. Then click on **Individual Years** in the main body of the page.

Look out for: This is a well-planned and splendidly illustrated outline of film history, decade-by-decade from the 1890s to 2001. Try **Pre-1920s Film History** about the birth of the cinema. Note the fine stills and posters. Click on a film title, such as **The Great Train Robbery** to get extra detail. Or go to the **1990s Film History** to hear about digital cinema, video and DVD.

Hints: A project on early cinema or silent cinema would be a good way to think about film as a medium.

Other links: Do some further research in this extensive site. There are a hundred great films in outline.

Student comments: A great site to explore!

Film: genre

How to use it • **Look out for** • **Hints** • **Other links** • **Student comments**

www.filmsite.org/genres.html

How to use it: Read the introduction to understand what film genre means. Then scroll down the alphabetically organised **Film Genres or Categories** table to find more detail.

Look out for: Try genres that appeal to you. **Animated Films**, for example, gives a lively history, with lovely coloured stills, from *Mickey Mouse* to *Shrek*. **War (Anti-war) Films** covers movies from *Hearts of the World* (1918) to *Saving Private Ryan* (1998). A title in blue gives you a more detailed commentary on that film. The posters are excellent.

Hints: Choose a genre and write about it, referring to three films from different eras.

Other links: www.bfi.org.uk/education
Lots more film information.

Student comments: I could go on looking through this for ever.

Film: study

How to use it | **Look out for** | **Hints** | **Other links** | **Student comments**

www.filmeducation.org

How to use it: Click on `Secondary Resources` and `Archive Menu`.

Look out for: The most useful sections for Key Stage 3 are `Great Expectations`, `Shakespeare on Screen` and `The Holocaust Memorial Day Resources`. You can compare the Dickens text and the film scenario, study scenes from *Macbeth*, directed by Polanski or Welles, and *Twelfth Night* directed by Trevor Nunn. The Holocaust Memorial Day Resources section lists relevant films – *Into the Arms of Strangers* offers moving resources related to children's experiences.

Hints: Use for Shakespeare SATs work, and for Anne Frank Day or for Holocaust study.

Other links: www.bfi.org.uk
More resources on film.

Comics

YEAR 7/8

- How to use it
- Look out for
- Hints
- Other links
- Student comments

www.bl.uk/collections/comics.html

How to use it: Scroll down and click on these three titles: **History of the Collection**, **Scope and Highlights of the Collection** and **Select List of British Comics**.

Look out for: This British Library site gives you many colourful front pages of historic comics. The history runs from *Funny Folks* (1874) to *Dandy* and *Beano* of today. It describes the comic characters that have meant so much to us, and explains the changes in design and audience. The comic list has lots of original front pages.

Hints: A history of the comic would be a valuable media study project. You'll need to look at some books noted here, too – especially those by Denis Gifford.

Other links: www.bl.uk/collections/football.html
More on popular culture: football magazines and programmes from 1898 onwards.

YEAR 8/9

Magazines

How to use it · **Look out for** · **Hints** · **Other links** · **Student comments**

www.teachit.co.uk

How to use it: Go to **Key Stage 3** and then to **Media & Non-fiction**. Click on **Investigating Magazines** and finally on **Teachit Online Lesson Pack**.

Look out for: This is a useful investigation of magazines and how they work in the market. Each section is a thorough, well-planned guide which makes you think – and work. The questions are probing, and technical terms are usefully explained. The discussions of language and presentation, such as **Front Covers**, are excellent.

Hints: Do the enjoyable activities on screen – you will learn a great deal! Then try making your own general interest magazine.

Other links: www.learn.co.uk
Go to **Reading Magazines** under **Key Stage 3 English Language**.

Student comments: I liked the Front covers section.

How to use it
Look out for
Hints
Other links
Student comments

YEAR 8/9

www.guardiancentury.co.uk

How to use it: Click on the decade required, or type in a year or a relevant phrase to find a particular story or event. When you find the article you want, click on red text to get more detail of each story.

Look out for: This *Guardian* newspaper archive is extremely full, useful and easy to use. The whole wealth of news reports from 1899 to 1999 is instantly at hand. Try the day after key dates of great events to get a full coverage, for example 5 August 1914, the outbreak of the Great War, 7 August 1945, the atomic bomb attack on Hiroshima, 23 November 1963, the assassination of President Kennedy, 1 September 1997, the death of Princess Diana.

Hints: After studying the language style, paragraph order and headlines of some great stories, make your own front page for one important 20th-century event.

Other links: www.bl.uk/collections/britnews.html
Short history of the British newspaper since 1620.

Student comments: It's a quick way to get into recent history.

Newspapers: history

Newspapers

YEAR 9

- How to use it
- Look out for
- Hints
- Other links
- Student comments

www.the-times.co.uk

How to use it: Explore the very full menu of news and features on the left of the page.

Look out for: This is the *The Times* online, impressive pages that are kept up-to-the-minute. Try **Breaking News** and **World** for the latest stories. What are the pop-up headlines for today? Read the leaders, then explore features like **Sport**, **Business**, **Arts**, or **Letters to the Editor** – under **Comment**.

Hints: Consider how a newspaper is balanced between informing and entertaining. Make two columns and choose items for each from *The Times*. Or compare this site with that of a popular tabloid (see below).

Other links:
www.mirror.co.uk
A best-selling popular paper.

Student comments: A smart, easy-to-use site. They must have people constantly typing!

Television: history

How to use it

Click on **British TV History**. Then go to **The Restored Video Recordings 1927–35**.

Look out for

A concise but thorough history of early television is given here. Above all, this unique site features the world's first television recordings by John Logie Baird. You catch glimpses of early television from the 1920s and 30s: Stookie Bill, the dummy that was the first TV image; a head turning; dancing girls; and the earliest TV play – *The Man with the Flower in his Mouth*.

Hints

This site is rather technical but the magical little moving images may inspire you to find out more about early television.

Other links

www.nmpft.org.uk
National Museum of Photography, Film and Television.

Student comments

The little recordings are unbelievable! TV has come a long way.

www.dfm.dircon.co.uk

YEAR 8/9

Television: soap operas

www.teachit.co.uk

How to use it: Go to **Key Stage 3**, then choose **Media & Non-fiction**. Click on **Soap Operas**.

Look out for: Soaps are an important and socially useful part of television. They are built into the lives of millions of people. There are some good, practical worksheets here: a letter to Points of View; an observation grid to help you analyse an episode; and a very full drama resource to help you and your friends create your own soap opera episode.

Hints: The sheets and activities will set you thinking. Try your own class survey of favourites. Follow this with the drama scheme.

Other links: soaps.about.com
Click on **British Soaps** to get to the individual sites.

Student comments: I love soaps and the drama is going to be fun.

How to use it | **Look out for** | **Hints** | **Other links** | **Student comments**

YEAR 8/9

news.bbc.co.uk

Television: news

Take your pick from the large array of items under (News Front Page). You can try audio or video for some articles.

This splendid BBC site will give you the very latest news. You get more instant news in more detail here than from any other online source. Try (Sport), for example: it has the latest scores, background and gossip. You can switch from TV to radio, or move to local news. You can join in discussion of issues and vote on controversial points. You can even see or hear certain items.

Compare this site with another like ITN or CBS, or look at this alongside newspaper sites such as those of *The Times* or the *Guardian*.

www.itn.co.uk

I'm going to use this one regularly, it's so good!

Radio: history

YEAR 8/9

www.bbc.co.uk/radio4/aboutradio4/history

How to use it
Read the introduction **Before Four** and then study the ten short chapters. Don't forget the broadcast example clips on the right-hand side. You can even take a **Visual Tour** around the studios.

Look out for
This is a very attractive, interesting site with its excellent short history of radio in Britain, and story of the growth of the BBC. We travel from Lord Reith in the 1920s to the top programmes of today. There are some striking details and valuable statistics. The radio clips, especially those from World War II, are fascinating.

Hints
Make a short study of the beginnings of radio in Britain. Include interviews with parents and grandparents about programmes they remember enjoying.

Other links
members.aol.com/jeff1070/script.html
A transcript of the famous *War of the Worlds* broadcast that caused a panic in the USA in 1938.

60

| How to use it | Look out for | Hints | Other links | Student comments |

YEAR 8/9

Radio

www.bbc.co.uk/radio

👆 Choose from the large menu on this page. Try looking at the various BBC radio stations or pick some of your favourite individual programmes.

👁 This is another excellent BBC page. Look into some of the special sites like **Woman's Hour** or **The Archers**. You can listen to past episodes, post messages or even vote about characters and plot. Explore the programmes you enjoy or look into new ones.

❗ Look at the **Today Programme** page. Watch it live and tour its studio. Prepare your own radio magazine programme about big issues in the news.

💻 Investigate the main links on this rich site.

💬 I never knew this existed. It's a good way to get more out of radio.

Propaganda

YEAR 9

How to use it · *Look out for* · *Hints* · *Other links* · *Student comments*

> www.firstworldwar.com/index.htm

Click on **Propaganda Posters**. Read the introduction and then click on **UK**.

The First World War created the first major advertising campaign. The combined attack of slogan, persuasive words and image was used to persuade volunteers to join up, and to tell civilians to continue the war effort. The campaign also stirred up hatred against the enemy. The posters on screen are rather small in size but you can read them and there is a fine collection here from several countries.

Try to analyse the persuasive methods of famous posters such as Your Country Wants You! (page 1), Are YOU in this? (page 1), Women of Britain Say Go! (page 2) and Daddy, What did YOU do in the Great War? (page 4). Then compare with the German posters.

www.ww1-propaganda-cards.com
More persuasion in postcard form.

A great site: lots of amazing propaganda.

Advertising

YEAR 8/9

How to use it | *Look out for* | *Hints* | *Other links* | *Student comments*

www.learn.co.uk

How to use it: Go to **Key Stage 3**, **English Language**. Scroll down to **Reading** and click on **Understanding Advertising**.

Look out for: There are many good sections in this general site on advertising technique. The units, noted in the menu on the left, are sharp in their questioning on topics like image, stereotyping and slogan. The **Language of Advertisers** is particularly valuable.

Hints: Don't miss the poem, *Attack on the Ad-Man* in the **Introduction to Advertising**! Do the exercises, then think about creating your own advertising leaflet. You could make one for your school, or the place where you live, for example.

Other links: www.teachit.co.uk
Much more about ads!

Student comments: Let's face it – adverts are great. This helps you to see how they work.

History of English

YEAR 7

How to use it · *Look out for* · *Hints* · *Other links* · *Student comments*

www.learn.co.uk

How to use it: Go to `Key Stage 3` `English Language` then try `Words, Words, Words` under `Language`. Click on `Word Origins`.

Look out for: You are given a short, nicely illustrated outline of the history of English from Celtic and Anglo-Saxon to the latest scientific and technical additions to the language. There are many interesting examples given for each major strand of language development. There is an interesting section on word origins.

Hints: Try the activities to support your learning, and check `Using a Dictionary` to find out more about etymology.

Other links: www.wordorigins.org/histeng.htm
Another good outline history.

English: history/variants

www.bbc.co.uk/radio4/routesofenglish

How to use it: Choose **Evolving English**, **Accents and Dialects** or **People and Places**. Click on **Go** for each one.

Look out for: This is Melvyn Bragg's fine radio series on the development of English. Evolving English discusses the history and spread of the language. You can follow the text on screen and hear sound clips in Accents and Dialects. Look at **No Pigeon** in **Series 3** about the most vibrant form of English heard in Brixton today!

Hints: This is a very rich site – use it to explore your own language interests. Perhaps you could do a study of English dialect and slang in your own area.

Other links:
www.eduseek.com
Find language variations.

Student comments: I enjoyed the slang and the sound clips.

Spelling

YEAR 7/8

How to use it | Look out for | Hints | Other links | Student comments

www.spelling.hemscott.net

Scroll down the first page to find a long list of spelling exercises. Read **Advice 1** and **Advice 2** first.

This thorough site gives plenty of reference and lots of exercises and puzzles. There is also advice for parents. The pages are very easy to read and well-presented, with helpful colour distinctions. Look at the points that everyone finds difficult, for example prefixes and suffixes, or the 'i before e' rule, and you'll see how good this site is.

Practise the exercises on each point, and try the puzzles and word-searches. They will certainly help you to improve!

www.teachit.co.uk
Spelling quiz from the NLS Framework list.

This is really clear and helpful.

Spelling

How to use it · **Look out for** · **Hints** · **Other links** · **Student comments**

www3.open.ac.uk/learners-guide/learning-skills/english

How to use it: Go to **The 'Tools' of Writing**. Scroll down to the three sections: **Spelling**, **Spelling Strategies** and **Some Useful Spelling Rules**.

Look out for: This is an expert guide with beautifully set-out pages. All the classic spelling strategies are here with lots of clear examples. The clarity and language style make this a good site but it can be difficult in places.

Hints: Make careful notes on the strategies and rules. If you write them yourself, you are more likely to remember them.

Other links: www.bradford.ac.uk/acad/civeng/skills/spelling.htm
Clear rules and mnemonics.

Student comments: This site isn't meant for people our age, so it's a good idea to make your own notes.

Punctuation

englishplus.com/grammar

How to use it: Scroll down and click on **Punctuation**. Choose the items that you want to study.

Look out for: The **Grammar Slammer** notes are full and clear and the colour coding helps you to follow them. **The Three Most Common Rules** helpfully focuses on the main ways in which commas should be used. If you can master these simple rules, you'll be correct most of the time! You'll need to know your parts of speech to get the most out of this – use the grammar glossary.

Hints: You may want to develop your punctuation skills by mastering the colon and the semi-colon, usually the least-known points. These notes will help.

Other links: www.eduseek.com
Choose **English** then do a search for **Punctuation**.

Student comments: This helped with my apostrophe problem.

Punctuation

How to use it — www3.open.ac.uk/learners-guide/learning-skills/english

Go to **The 'Tools' of Writing** and then click on **Punctuation**.

Look out for — This is intended for older students who have missed out on good teaching but you will find it useful, too. Read the introduction and then scroll through the points by clicking **Next**. The notes are clear with good examples in coloured boxes. The basics, and the harder ideas, are all here. Again, it's best if you know your parts of speech.

Hints — Test the site by checking on your least favourite points: apostrophes, commas and colons or semi-colons. Try the **Activity** pages to check your progress.

Other links — www.tc.cc.va.us/writcent/HANDOUTS/grammar/index.htm
Another clear guide.

Student comments — I've made my own notes on this site so that I really take it in.

Grammar: parts of speech

YEAR 7/8

- How to use it
- Look out for
- Hints
- Other links
- Student comments

www.learn.co.uk

How to use it: Go to **Key Stage 3** **English Language**. Then click on **Parts of speech**. Read the **Lesson Objectives** and follow the menu.

Look out for: Everyone needs to know about the parts of speech and how they are used. The pictorial guide is amusing and helpful. Check the parts you know least well, such as prepositions. Then look closely at nouns, adjectives, etc. This is excellent for revision if you already know something about parts of speech.

Hints: Have a go at some of the lively activities suggested in each section. They are easy to do but will reinforce the rules.

Other links: englishplus.com/grammar
More valuable reference.

Student comments: I'm glad I've sorted out adverbs and adjectives at last.

Sentences

YEAR 7/8

www.learn.co.uk

How to use it: Go to **Key Stage 3** **English Language**. Then click on **Sentences**. Work your way down the menu on the left.

Look out for: Writing correct sentences is the key to success in English. This site takes you through all aspects of the sentence: the different kinds of clauses and phrases, word order and the main verbs. It's so lively and well-presented that you can't help making progress.

Hints: Enjoy doing the self-marking activities that will allow you to see your progress.

Other links: www.askoxford.com
Answers your questions about English usage.

Student comments: This straightened out some points that I found difficult.

Grammar: general

YEAR 8/9

- How to use it
- Look out for
- Hints
- Other links
- Student comments

englishplus.com/grammar

How to use it: Go to `Style and Usage`, then click on `Sentence Fragments`.

Look out for: These notes are well-planned and easy to use. There are explanations of subjects, verbs, plus main and subordinate clauses. The underlined words are explained in the glossary. It may seem difficult, but it's vital if you want to reach the higher levels in the SATs.

Hints: In the main menu, the section on `Common Mistakes and Choices` is very helpful. Here are classic problems like 'a lot', 'all right', 'between/among' and many others. Now you can get them sorted out!

Other links: www.worldwide.edu/ci/usa/grammar.html
Lots more grammar links.

Student comments: The Common Mistakes page is good. I know I make lots of these!

Dictionary

YEAR All

- How to use it
- Look out for
- Hints
- Other links
- Student comments

www.dictionary.com

How to use it: Go to `Ask Doctor Dictionary`. You can also look up other sites on this title page.

Look out for: Doctor Dictionary is fun. Simply type in the word that you want to know about – I tried 'simile'. An explanation of simile and some clear examples came up as easy-to read, full notes. Move on to `Fun & Games` with its crosswords and word searches. You can certainly increase your word power here!

Hints: There are other stimulating word games on these pages. Dip into them.

Other links:
www.askoxford.com
More about words – and some games and puzzles.

Student comments: Dr. Dictionary is faster than going through a book.

Dictionary of literature

YEAR 8/9

How to use it | Look out for | Hints | Other links | Student comments

www.glossarist.com

Go to **Arts and Culture**, then to **Literature**. Choose from the list – most useful will be the **Glossary of Poetic Terms**, **Glossary of Literary Terms**, **RhymeZone**, **Bibliomania** and **Fantastic Fiction Bibliographies**.

This is a challenging site but it is packed with the solid information that you need when studying literature. Build up your own list of literary terms as you develop their use in your writing. You'll enjoy RhymeZone and Fantastic Fiction, where I looked up Mary Shelley and found a feast of Frankenstein!

Use as background reference for all kinds of work connected with literature.

I'm gradually getting to know some literary terms so this site has been very useful.

Thesaurus

YEAR: All

- How to use it
- Look out for
- Hints
- Other links
- Student comments

www.wordsmyth.net

How to use it: Simply type your chosen word into the box, then click **Define it**.

Look out for: Speed and clarity are the best features of this combined thesaurus and dictionary. The word is defined, and you are told which part of speech it is and what are its variant forms. Many synonyms are offered (but not antonyms). Quick, clear and very useful. American and English spellings are given.

Hints: Try out a few words just for practice, then use this site regularly in your own writing.

Other links: www.bartleby.com
The updated, full *Roget's Thesaurus*.

Student comments: I find the book of *Roget's Thesaurus* confusing. This site was easier to use.

Encyclopedia

YEAR All

- How to use it
- Look out for
- Hints
- Other links
- Student comments

www.encyclopedia.com

How to use it: Select the initial letter of your chosen topic or enter your **Keyword** into the box. You might also find the **Reference Desk** useful.

Look out for: This is the free online version of the *Columbia Encyclopedia*. I searched on 'Shakespeare' and found 263 connected sites packed with useful facts and dates.

Hints: This is a good place to start your research and it is free!

Other links: Move to the dictionaries, thesauruses, almanacs and additional encyclopedias listed on the main page.

Student comments: Book encyclopedias are massive and we don't have one at home so this site suits me.

Great writers

www.lib.lsu.edu/hum/authors.html

How to use it: Read the preface to find out what the site does. Then scroll down the list of authors until you find the one you want.

Look out for: This is a valuable guide to websites about great authors. It is written at quite a high level but you will find appropriate material about writers whom you study in school. Try Austen, Dickens, Doyle, Mary Shelley or Tolkien and, of course, Shakespeare. There are some strange omissions: the Brontës and Wordsworth, for example.

Hints: There are so many useful things here to help enrich your literary study projects.

Other links: www.people.virginia.edu/~jbh/author.html
Another fine author site.

Student comments: I'm working on Arthur Conan Doyle so this is going to help me.

YEAR 8/9

SATs: reading

www.bbc.co.uk/education/ks3bitesize

(How to use it) Under **Choose a Subject** select **Reading Fiction** and click. Choose from the menu. Later you can come back to this point to look at **Reading Non-Fiction**, which covers fact and opinion, and persuasive language.

(Look out for) The notes deal with character, language and sentences – try them all. You are offered general statements that could apply to any fiction. The language points on vocabulary, imagery and atmosphere are the most interesting because they include examples of texts.

(Hints) The tests are particularly good for revision, and you can keep repeating them to check on your progress.

(Other links) www.learn.co.uk
This includes a file of SATs papers.

(Student comments) Reading is my SATs weakness so I was grateful for the tests.

SATs: writing

www.bbc.co.uk/education/ks3bitesize

How to use it: Under **Choose a Subject**, select **Writing**. Look at the detailed menus to choose topics and tests.

Look out for: This is an attractive site written in friendly language. It covers topics thoroughly – sentence structure is a key point.

Hints: Do the tests patiently. If you go wrong, just try again. They are excellent for revision. Try **Writing a Speech** or **Writing an Article – Persuasive Writing**.

Other links: www.channel4.com/learning/secondary.html
More SATs advice.

SATs: general

YEAR 9

How to use it | *Look out for* | *Hints* | *Other links* | *Student comments*

www.learn.co.uk

Go to **Key Stage 3** **English Language** and choose from the **Language**, **Writing** and **Reading** menus.

Detailed notes cover every aspect of the Key Stage 3 English SATs. This site is very useful for those aiming at higher levels – it is strongest on the various kinds of writing you will need to do in the tests. Look at the excellent notes on **Writing to Persuade**, for example. Old papers are also available here.

During Year 9, try some of the tasks that have been carefully set out here. They are quite challenging and enjoyable.

www.teachit.co.uk/teachit/sats.htm
Lots more teacher-written material.

I think this site is hard but it's probably the best one for SATs.

Vocabulary

YEAR 7/8

How to use it · Look out for · Hints · Other links · Student comments

www.rhymezone.com

How to use it: Enter a word, select **Find Rhymes** and click **Go Get it!** to see the wide range of word exploration here.

Look out for: Here is a site to help with vocabulary – and with your poems, too. There is a rhyming dictionary, a thesaurus function and the word quizzes are challenging and fun. You might find a use for the quotations from Shakespeare and the Bible. Beware of American spellings!

Hints: If you like writing rhymed poems, this will be very useful, even if some of the rhymes are far-fetched.

Other links: www.dictionary.com

Student comments: This is brilliant for poems – and it's so fast!

Vocabulary: skills

YEAR 7

How to use it — *Look out for* — *Hints* — *Other links* — *Student comments*

www.learn.co.uk

How to use it: Go to **Key Stage 3**, **English Language**. Then go to **Words, Words, Words** under **Language** and choose **Building Vocabulary Skills** and **Synonyms and Antonyms**.

Look out for: In Building Vocabulary Skills, there is good advice about words that express the subtle shades and textures of meaning in English. The exercises based on a thesaurus are fresh and easy to follow. Synonyms and antonyms are also well-explored.

Hints: The activities are interesting to do and are quite stretching so that you can check your understanding.

Other links:
www.dictionary.com
Try Dr. Dictionary.

Student comments: This site is huge! All the exercises in this section are fun.

82

Word origins

www.geocities.com/etymonline

How to use it: After you have read the **Introduction**, click on the first letter of your chosen word. Then go to the more detailed letter guide. Do look up what any abbreviations in the definition mean – there is a long list, e.g. L = Latin.

Look out for: Etymology is the study of where words come from. The author claims to have produced the only full online dictionary of word origins. The letter menu and clear print make this site very quick to use. I looked up parliament (Old French: *parler*), sofa (Arabic) and university (Latin) to try the system.

Hints: Use in relation to any study you make of the history of English.

Other links:
www.wordorigins.org
Another interesting etymology site.

Student comments: It's good to know how old words are and where they came from.

YEAR All

Sentence construction

YEAR: All

- **How to use it** 🔌
- **Look out for** 👁
- **Hints** ❗
- **Other links** 💻
- **Student comments** 💬

> www.shared-visions.com/explore/english/english.html

🔌 On the Exploring English title page, click on **Menu for the Parts of Speech**. Then go to all three sections: **Anatomy Chart, Parts of Speech** and **Sentences**.

👁 This crisp, colourful and well-designed site reminds you about grammar basics. Start with the excellent Anatomy Chart, Parts of Speech – well worth copying into your notes. The **Sentences** section deals with various types of sentence structure. You'll need to know about clauses and phrases to be able to follow this properly.

❗ Test yourself on parts of speech and then learn the variety of sentence construction. You'll need to be aware of this material to reach higher levels in the SATs.

💻 www.learn.co.uk
More about sentences.

💬 I learned a lot on this site.

Paragraphs

www2.actden.com/writ_den/tips/paragrap

How to use it: Choose from the lists: **Parts of a Paragraph**, **How to Write a Paragraph**, **Kinds of Paragraphs**.

Look out for: The site will help you to shape your ideas effectively. **Topic Sentence**, **Supporting Details** and **Closing Sentence** sound mechanical but can be used in factual essays in all school subjects. Good, full examples are given. The five writing stages are vital and various kinds of paragraphs are fully covered.

Hints: Preparation and checking are excellently done here. Make careful notes from the list of points.

Other links: www.paragraphpunch.com
A more interactive instruction site.

Student comments: It's a plain site but it does give good advice.

Style

www.bartleby.com/141

Read the text about **The Elements of Style**, which is a famous book guide. Choose from the list of **Contents**.

This is not easy material but it is clear and expert. One of its authors was that wonderful writer, E.B. White, who created *Charlotte's Web*. Do you wonder whether to add a possessive apostrophe to a name ending in s? Here is a classic answer. You'll need to know your parts of speech to get the best out of this advice. It covers sentences, paragraphs, punctuation and spelling in relation to good style.

Don't try to read all of this. Just refer to points you find confusing – and make notes on them! The site will certainly help with SATs writing.

www.wsu.edu:8080/~brians/errors/index.html
A guide to common errors.

This is a good place to get answers for writing problems.

Standard English

How to use it | **Look out for** | **Hints** | **Other links** | **Student comments**

www.learn.co.uk

🔌 Go to **Key Stage 3** **English Language**. Then go to **Speaking and Listening** and **Appropriate Talk**.

👁 Explore the menu of units. The section **We all sound different** deals with accent and pronunciation – there are useful definitions here. Then move on to **Using Standard English**. You are invited to act out scenes to illustrate the ideas.

❗ Try **Activities 1** and **Activities 2** under **Accents and Dialects**. Enjoy the dialect poem *Dahn the Plug 'Ole*.

🖥 www.eduseek.com
Click on **Standard English**.

💬 This site is colourful and funny. It makes dull-looking ideas interesting.

Reading for research

YEAR 7/8

- How to use it
- Look out for
- Hints
- Other links
- Student comments

> www.shunsley.eril.net/armoore/engks3/research.htm

How to use it: Read the **Introduction** before making your selections.

Look out for: This is a thoughtful general guide to reading. There are ideas about making notes, (including using a 'scratchpad'), choosing a subject, and gathering information from books, broadcast and electronic media. 'Do not simply copy' is the sensible key idea! There are also sound points about presentation and style.

Hints: Print out this page to keep, or write your own careful notes from it. It is an ambitious site and will come in useful for various school projects.

Other links: Reading the non-fiction section on this site will give you more ideas.

How to use it **Look out for** **Hints** **Other links** **Student comments**

Reading for meaning

> www.learn.co.uk

Go to **Key Stage 3** **English Language**, then choose **Reading for Meaning – Part 1** and **Part 2**.

Read the **Introduction** carefully. These are demanding but interesting lessons, dealing with ideas like style, prediction or deducing meaning. Difficult words are well-explained – just click on them. The passages from *Wuthering Heights* and *Oliver Twist* keep you close to real writing, and the exercises are interactive so that you learn fast.

Work your way through the passages and exercises. There is a lot to do but you will find it stimulating.

Try **Reading Strategies** on this same site.

This was stretching and interesting.

Writer's craft

www.learn.co.uk

How to use it

Go to **Key Stage 3** **English Language – Prose**. Then work your way through the menu under **Exploring Prose**.

Look out for

This is a valuable introduction to the prose writer's craft. There are important study areas here, for example story, plot, theme and narrative voice. Useful diagrams support the main ideas. The notes on **Setting and Atmosphere** are particularly effective, especially in the nine-step analysis of a novel extract. The best sections deal with authorial voice and irony.

Hints

The activities are lively and pleasant to do on screen. There is plenty to interest you and make you learn.

Other links

www.englishbiz.co.uk/mainguides/fiction.htm
Detailed discussion of narrative.

Student comments

You can learn a lot in a short time and then apply it to the book you're reading.

Studying texts

YEAR 7

www.shunsley.eril.net/armoore/engks3/reading.htm

How to use it
Click on **Basic Guide**.

Look out for
A clear page describing the various written responses that you might make to books you have read. It gives you a structure of introduction, characters, settings and verdict. Or you might try a more imaginative approach with retelling episodes, writing a sequel or prequel, or doing a magazine or TV review.

Hints
These excellent notes are worth copying for reference. They apply to any general wide reading book report that you may have to do, giving you the right shape and practical ideas for getting started.

Other links
www.learn.co.uk
Try **Exploring Prose** under **Key Stage 3** **English Literature – Prose**.

Student comments
I used this outline with my review of *Treasure Island*.

Writing: planning/drafting

How to use it — **Look out for** — **Hints** — **Other links** — **Student comments**

> owl.english.purdue.edu/handouts/general/index.html

How to use it: Click on the four-part contents display. Start with `Planning/Starting to Write`, then work through the detailed menu.

Look out for: The Owl Online Writing Lab is an American university site but there is a lot here that is helpful for you. The language is friendly and the points are practical. For example, in planning: you can brainstorm, nutshell your idea, diagram it, write a draft and return to it later. It's all useful. There are also some excellent strategies for proof-reading.

Hints: Read the site through and make notes on what is appropriate for your use.

Other links: writing.richmond.edu/writing/wweb.html

Student comments: The planning ideas are just what I need.

Writing to imagine

How to use it | **Look out for** | **Hints** | **Other links** | **Student comments**

www.learn.co.uk

Go to **Key Stage 3**, **English Language**, then click on **Writing to Imagine**.

This is a good site for story writing. It reminds you about key words, such as setting and plot. **Using Your Senses** will help you to create a descriptive setting, while **Continuing a Story** asks you to develop story starters from passages by well-known authors.
Creating a Legend is a fine climax.

The activities, some of which can be done on-screen, are attractive and worthwhile.
Write a Legend is the best task, with its careful, detailed instruction.

www.teachit.co.uk
Two good sites on story openings and endings.

Writing to inform

How to use it | **Look out for** | **Hints** | **Other links** | **Student comments**

www.learn.co.uk

How to use it: Go to **Key Stage 3**, **English Language**, then click on **Writing to Inform**.

Look out for: This is a good general guide to informative writing, reminding you about tone, language level and layout. Move into **Writing for the Newspaper**. Roll over the article as you read it to get more information about its features. You can then do the same for **Writing a Magazine Article**. The reminders in **Writing a Formal Letter** are also helpful.

Hints: All the activities are well-prepared and interesting to do, especially those on the newspaper and magazine articles.

Other links: www.englishbiz.co.uk/mainguides/inform.htm

Student comments: Good activities.

Writing to persuade

www.englishbiz.co.uk/mainguides/persuade.htm

🖱️ Go to **Persuade** at the top of the page and scroll through the points.

👁️ This is really aimed at GCSE level but it will help also with Key Stage 3 – good guides on this topic are rare! Remind yourself what persuasion is and then look over the points on rhetoric. The excellent ideas from **How Can I Do it Well?** will guide you effectively. Think about audience, purpose and the form of your writing.

❗ The **Plan**, **Write**, **Check** sections provide good revision. Make careful notes on structure, rhetorical devices and connectives.

🖥️ www.learn.co.uk
A short guide to persuasion. You have to create a dialogue and a leaflet.

💬 I now see what I'm supposed to do with this sort of writing.

Writing to review

YEAR 8/9

- How to use it
- Look out for
- Hints
- Other links
- Student comments

film.guardian.co.uk

How to use it: Scroll down the central column to find new film titles that interest you and click on the title.

Look out for: This excellent review site gives you the facts about the film, describes its content and shows you film stills. You can read what the critics thought of it under **Reviews** and link to some official film sites.

Hints: Blend the whole range of facts and commentary to produce your own review of a film that you have enjoyed recently.

Other links: www.allmovie.com
Another good guide to films. Don't miss the classics like *Frankenstein*.

Student comments: I love films and this guide really helps you to do a review.

Speaking and listening

YEAR 7/8

- How to use it
- Look out for
- Hints
- Other links
- Student comments

www.learn.co.uk

How to use it: Go to **Key Stage 3**, **English Language**. Then choose **Speaking and Listening**.

Look out for: This is a beautifully planned resource, full of good ideas and advice. **Appropriate Talk** is a good way to begin with its reminders about Standard English and its variations. The play scripts and acted stories are obviously fun. Move on to the other sections under Speaking and Listening, which will help you speak, discuss and – importantly – listen more effectively.

Hints: Go into the activities sections for lively follow-up to the explanations. You can view sample answers to check your progress.

Other links: Explore further links on this huge site.

Student comments: I'm a bit shy so I'm glad to get help with speaking and listening.

Great speeches

www.pbs.org/greatspeeches

Go to **Speech Archive**, then choose by era, clicking on particular dates.

There are some wonderful, important speeches on this impressive American site. You can also actually hear and see excerpts from the speeches themselves. Click on **Background** for more information about the speakers. Try **Franklin Roosevelt Declares War** (1941), **John Kennedy Blasts Communism** (1963) or **Martin Luther King's 'I have a Dream'** speech (1963).

Go to **Ideas for Teachers** for some excellent exercises comparing great speeches. The guide also deals with rhetoric and presenting an argument.

www.historychannel.com/speeches
More fine speeches on all kinds of topics.

This is so exciting. I just wish there were more British speeches.

Discussion

| How to use it | Look out for | Hints | Other links | Student comments |

YEAR 7/8

www.learn.co.uk

How to use it: Go to **Key Stage 3**, **English Language**. Then under **Speaking and Listening** choose **Discussing Effectively**.

Look out for: Some of you will find discussion difficult and this site gives you practical help. Start with **Participate Like a Pro**. Which sort of creature are you in discussion: elephant, monkey, mouse or lion? Run the cursor over the pictures to find out! Then move to **Getting Agreement**, where you find useful ideas on the conduct of discussion.

Hints: It's a good idea to make written notes from the **Tips** section of this interesting site.

Other links: Move to **Listening Effectively** on the same site.

English: general

www.eduseek.com

How to use it: Choose **English**, then select the age group. Go to **English Language** or **English Literature**.

Look out for: The headings are clear and the material is up-to-date. There is a vast choice of links on this massive site. English is well-handled and English literature has some good links – on multi-cultural poetry, war poetry and lots on Shakespeare.

Hints: Use this site as a starter for all sorts of topics. It takes you deeper and deeper…

Other links:
www.educationindex.com
Click **Subject** and then go to **Literature** for much useful material.

Student comments: Make a special note of this site as it covers so many things.

| How to use it | Look out for | Hints | Other links | Student comments | YEAR All |

vlmp.museophile.com/uk.html

- Click on the first letter of your chosen museum or gallery. Then click on the title of the museum for general information about it.

- This site will be valuable in any literary history project that you undertake. I found some favourites: the **Dickens House Museum** and **Jane Austen's House**, **MOMI**, the **Brontë Parsonage**, **Shakespeare** and the **Globe**. They're all here, and the site saves you hunting around.

- Use with imagination to follow up background research on authors and themes.

- www.24hourmuseum.org.uk
  Lots more about national museums.

- A great site that will help with English and other school subjects.

Published by Letts Educational
The Chiswick Centre
414 Chiswick High Road
London W4 5TF
020 89963333
020 87428390
mail@lettsed.co.uk
www.letts-education.com

Letts Educational is part of the Granada Learning Group.
Granada Learning is a division of Granada plc.
© Christopher Martin 2003

First published 2003

ISBN 184085 8818

The author asserts the moral right to be identified as the author of this work.

All rights reserved. No part of this publication may be reproduced, stored in a retrieval system, or transmitted in any form or by any means, electronic, mechanical, photocopying, recording or otherwise, without either the prior permission of the Publisher or a licence permitting restricted copying in the United Kingdom issued by the Copyright Licensing Agency Ltd, 90 Tottenham Court Road, London W1P 9HE. This book is sold subject to the condition that it shall not by way of trade or otherwise be lent, hired out or otherwise circulated without the publisher's prior consent.

All web addresses are correct at the time of going to press. The information in this book has been thoroughly researched and checked for accuracy. Safety advice is given where appropriate. Neither the authors nor the publishers can accept responsibility for any loss or damage incurred as a result of this book.

British Library Cataloguing in Publication Data
A catalogue record for this book is available from the British Library.

Acknowledgements
The publishers would like to thank the following for permission to use copyright material. Every effort has been made to trace copyright holders and to obtain their permission for the use of copyright material. The author and publishers will gladly receive information enabling them to rectify any error or omission in subsequent editions.

Commissioned by Helen Clark
Project management by Vicky Butt
Editorial by Kearsey & Finn Limited
Design and production © Gecko Limited, Bicester, Oxon
Illustrations by © Gecko Limited, Bicester, Oxon
Production by PDQ
Printed and bound by Ashford Colour Press